WORDSWORTH AND THE FAMOUS LORTON YEW TREE

Subscribers

Charles Allison

S Balogh

Sally Birch

Tom Bird

Elizabeth Birkett

Wolfgang Bopp
Curator, Hillier's
Arboretum

Ian Brodie

John Brookman

M E Burkett

Mrs Cockton

Bevis Cubey

Janet Cubey
Prin Botanist RHS

Hunter Davies

Sheila J Drewery
née Cunningham

Eric N C Eustance

Anne Flower

Janet Graham

Michael Grieve

Richard Hall

Tirril Harris

Diane Hassell

Hiley family

D & R Hill

Mrs D R Holbrook

John Hudson

Judy Hudson

Victoria Jay

Alan R Johnson

Kathryn W Johnson

Iris Johnston

Christine Judd

Frank Judd

Laurence Kelly

D Kennon

Madelaine Kerr

Kirkgate Centre Museum

Lorton School

Betty Marshall

Jeremy Over

Ann Carol Parker

Roger Peck

D R Pelly

Ben Poate

Charles Poate

Christine Poate

Tim Poate

Alison Pomphret
in memory of
Frank Johnston

Enid Pomphret
née Johnston

R Ratcliffe

Stephen Revell

Anne Revell

Ann Roberts

Mrs Dorothy Robinson

Dr Quentin Robinson

Bev Rowland

Elly Rowland

Scale Hill, Loweswater

Sandra Shaw

Pauline Stables

Mike Suckling

Julian Thurgood

Catherine Tolley

Margaret Wardley

Pat Williams

Wordsworth and the famous Lorton yew tree

Edited by
Michael G Baron
Derek Denman

Lorton & Derwent Fells Local History Society
September 2004

Front and back covers: *The yew tree at Lorton*, photographs by David Herrod, 2004

Inside front and back covers: *Yew-Trees*, facsimile from *Poems 1815* by William Wordsworth, courtesy of the Wordsworth Trust

Copyright © 2004, Lorton & Derwent Fells Local History Society
All rights reserved. This book may not be reproduced in whole or in part, stored in a retrieval system or transmitted in any form, except by reviewers for the Press, without written permission from the publisher and copyright holder

First published in 2004

Published and distributed by the Lorton and Derwent Fells
Local History Society
www.derwentfells.com

Printed in Great Britain by Titus Wilson, Kendal

ISBN 0-9548487-0-5

Contents

Preface Dr Robert Woof	vii
Introduction	1
The Lorton yew tree in early records	3
The Wordsworths' visit in 1804	7
The poem	11
The Lorton yew tree in guidebooks and histories from 1800	19
The life of the Lorton yew tree	41
Photographs for the bicentenary David Herrod	43
A poem for the bicentenary Jacob Polley	49
The common yew John Spedding	51
'A famous yew-tree' Canon H D Rawnsley 1903	55
Contributors	65
Bibliography	66
Subscribers	69

Preface

Dr Robert Woof – Director, The Wordsworth Trust

A landscape with a ruin, preferably a picturesque ruin, is quintessentially a Romantic image. It embodies a sense of history, a sense of loss, and yet indicates strength to survive. For Wordsworth, if there were not some marks of human intervention in a landscape, he would feel a profound alienation. For him, there had to be a relationship between the mind and the place: 'The mind of man is married to this goodly universe'. So, for Wordsworth, this marriage was something that centred the human being, giving a focus for the human heart which, in turn, had its centre on the hearth, on family life.

In 1800, drafting some lines for his poem *Michael*, he explains that he needed to see 'some vestiges of human hands, some stirs / Of human passion.' Such vestiges, he says:

> to me are sweet
> As light at sunbreak, or the sudden sound
> Of music to a blind man's ear who sits
> Alone and silent in summer shade.

He then makes great claims for these 'vestiges of human hands', these 'stirs of human passions':

> They are as a creation in my heart;
> I look into past times as prophets look
> Into futurity, a stream of life runs back
> Into dead years, the porticoes of thought,
> The lyric spirit of philosophy
> Leads me through moods of sadness to delight.

Wordsworth feels the imperative to link the present with its rich past. But, when the link can be made through a tree – a venerable yew tree – the tree represents a living ruin. It presents an even more triumphant emblem of something that outlasts our actual and human history.

The yew tree at Lorton was not the first of 'single' trees that he writes about in his poetry. In the 'Ode: Intimations of Immortality' he gives us the idea that the tree presents a keen but sweet interruption into the joy that he had felt on 'this sweet May-morning':

> But there's Tree of many one,
> A single Field which I have looked upon,
> Both of them speak of something that is gone . . .

But again, even more memorably in the *Prelude*, book sixth, he describes 'a single tree' which he had known in the land adjoining St. John's College, Cambridge, where he went as an undergraduate in 1787. The tree is an ash tree, seen in winter, but miraculously brought to life by tassels and festoons of ivy:

> trunk and master branches every where
> Were green with ivy, and the lightsome twigs
> And outer spray profusely tipped with seeds
> That hung in yellow tassels and festoons,
> Moving or still – a favourite trimmed out
> By winter for himself . . .

This tree in winter is made alive by the 'outlandish grace' of the ivy, whose nature is to raise itself so that it can flower in the sunlight at the top of the tree.

When Wordsworth writes of the Lorton Yew, he finds in the great tree an image that combines the span of years with the idea of heroic survival: an extravagant claim for the immortality of the tree:

> This solitary Tree! A living thing
> Produced too slowly ever to decay;
> Of form and aspect too magnificent
> To be destroyed.

Wordsworth commands his readers to admire a wonder. He seeks to give us, once again, intimations of immortality. He seems to claim that this tree produced in slow time even allows us to question the reality of death (which may merely be a skeleton), or of time (reduced simply to a shadow).

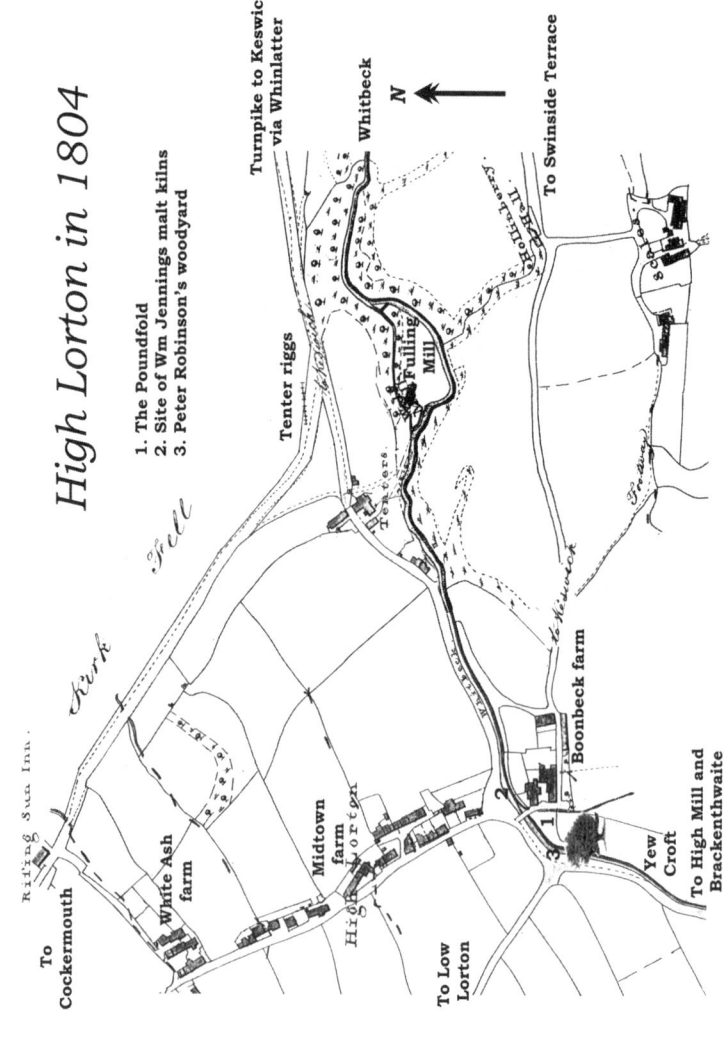

Introduction

Look at it now, and think of it no longer as a broken yew-tree, sown here perchance by some far wandering bird centuries ago, but as a living witness ... Canon H D Rawnsley, *Lake Country Sketches*, 1903

From a measurement taken in the 1820s we know that the Lorton yew tree was then a much larger tree, having grown with the village during its early history. When William and Dorothy Wordsworth came to Lorton Vale in late September 1804 the tree was a magnificent sight. Already it was a famous yew tree, one of a few in Cumberland. George Fox, the Quaker preacher, had noted a yew tree 'full of people' in his Journal for 1653, but did not name the village.

2004 is the bicentenary of the Wordsworths' making a six-day tour from Grasmere to Seathwaite in the Duddon valley. One object of the tour was to visit a yew tree in Lorton Vale. The visit is inextricably linked with William Wordsworth's poem *Yew-trees*, published in 1815. The first part of the poem describes the tree and puts its useful wood and longevity into the context of English history on the Border and in the Hundred Years' War. Why they made this special visit, and whether the poem was conceived then, or later, or earlier as Wordsworth recalled in his seventies, are still open questions, to which tentative answers appear on pages 11-13.

Nonetheless, whatever academic opinion says, the poem, the natural world, the Wordsworths, the Lake District, are inevitably and forever associated with the yew tree. Lorton Vale becomes a minor, but real, place on the enduring map of English Romanticism; a place, too, where poetry aligns with geography, history and ancient trees.

There are two subjects in this book – the tree and the poem. The year 2004 provides an opportunity to revisit both.

Much of the content is the collected writings of guides and historians of the nineteenth century. Tourism to the Lake District is growing. The reputations of the Lake Poets – Wordsworth, Coleridge and to a lesser extent Southey, are well established. Soon, in the 1840s, railways will come, and curious visitors will knock on Wordsworth's door at Rydal Mount. The more adventurous will come to Lorton, too. As to the tree, sadly there is no picture of it in its 1804 'pride'. Included here are the later illustrations. The historical content stops at 1912, with the publication of *Wordsworth's Birthplace*, by John Bolton, Lorton Vale's first local historian. The bibliography contains details of relevant books.

Without the generosity and help of the Wordsworth Trust and its staff, and their permission to reproduce material from their unique archive, this book might not have been published. It is right that the Preface has been written by the Director, Dr Robert Woof, CBE. Arboriculture is represented by a discourse on the species, invited from John Spedding, CBE, of Mirehouse, and President of the Royal Forestry Society. The new photographs are by David Herrod, well known for his landscape pictures and publications. And to mark the bicentenary, we have commissioned a new poem by Carlisle's 'Next Generation' poet Jacob Polley.

We are also grateful to other individuals and organisations who have supplied material, research or who have helped with the production. Our subscribers, some of whom are listed from page 69, supported by placing orders. Grants to assist publication were made by the Cockermouth & District Neighbourhood Forum and the lottery-based 'Awards for All' – without them, too, *Wordsworth and the famous Lorton yew tree* would have been a blank page, a missed opportunity.

The Lorton yew tree in early records

George Fox, 1653

George Fox, the Quaker preacher, is believed to be the first to make reference to the Lorton yew tree in early 1653, in the Commonwealth period. As a young man of 28, he preached at many meetings in Cumberland and spent time in Carlisle gaol. His journal, first published in 1694, makes particular reference to a yew tree:

> 'Now was I moved to send James Lancaster to appoint a meeting at John Wilkinson's steeplehouse near COCKERMOUTH, who was a preacher in great repute, and had three parishes under him; wherefore I stayed at Millom-in-Bootle till he came back again. In the meantime some of those called the gentry of the country had formed a plot against me, and had given a little boy a rapier, to do me a mischief with it. They came with the boy to Joseph Nicholson's house to seek me; but the Lord had so ordered it, that I was gone into the fields. They met with James Lancaster but did not much abuse him; and not finding me in the house, after a while they went away again. So I walked up and down in the fields that night, and did not go to bed as very often I used to do. The next day we came to the steeple-house, where James Lancaster had appointed the meeting. There were at this meeting twelve soldiers and their wives, who were come thither from Carlisle; and the country people came in, as if it had been to a fair. I lay at a house a short distance from the place, so that many Friends were there before me. **When I came, I found James Lancaster speaking under a yew tree; which was so full of people that I feared they would break it down.** I looked about for a place to stand upon, to speak to the people; for they lay all

Supposed portrait of George Fox, 1677, in *Quaker Meeting* by Egbert van Heemskerk

up and down like people at a leaguer. After I was discovered, a professor came to me, and asked, if I would not go into the church; seeing no place convenient to speak to the people from, I told him, "Yes"; whereupon the people rushed in; so that when I came in, the house and even the pulpit was so full of people, that I had much ado to get in; and they that could not get in, stood about the walls. When the people were settled, I stood up on a seat; and the Lord opened my mouth "to declare his everlasting truth, and his everlasting day; and to lay open all their teachers, their rudiments, traditions, and inventions, that they had been in, in the night of apostacy since the apostles' days. I turned them to Christ the true teacher, and to the true spiritual worship; directing them where to find the Spirit and truth, that they might worship God therein. I opened Christ's parables unto them, and directed them to the Spirit of God *in* themselves, that would open the Scriptures unto them. And I showed them, how all might come to know their Saviour, and sit under his teaching; might come to be heirs of the kingdom of God, and know both the voice of God and of Christ, by which they might discover all the false shepherds and teachers they had been under; and be gathered to the true shepherd, priest, bishop, and prophet, Christ Jesus, whom God commanded all to hear." So when I had largely declared the word of life unto them, for about three hours, I walked from amongst the people, and they passed away very well satisfied. Among the rest a professor followed me, praising and commending me; but his words were like a thistle to me. At last I turned about, and bid him "fear the Lord": whereupon priest Larkham, of Cockermouth (for several priests were got together on the way who came after the meeting was over), said to me, "Sir, why do you judge so; you must not judge." But I turned to him and said, "Friend, dost not thou discern an exhortation from a judgment? I admonished him to fear God; and dost thou say I judge him?" So this priest and I falling into discourse, I manifested him to be amongst the false prophets and covetous hirelings. And several people being moved to speak to him, he and two others of the priests soon got away. When they were gone, John Wilkinson, who was preacher of that parish, and of two other parishes in Cumberland, began to dispute against his own conscience for several hours, till the people generally turned against him; for he thought to have tired me out, but the Lord's power tired him out, and the Lord's truth came over him and them all. Many hundreds were convinced that day, and received the Lord Jesus Christ, and his free teaching, with gladness; of whom some have died in the truth, and many stand faithful witnesses thereof. The soldiers also were convinced, and their wives, and continued with me till First-day.'

From the itinerary given in the journal, it is clear that these events take place in either Lorton or Embleton, and it is only the yew tree that indicates Lorton. Some Quaker testimonies of

1705-1710, however, place the events in Embleton, without mentioning the tree. While it is likely that the tree George Fox saw was in Lorton, it is possible that the church was at Lorton or Embleton, or that both were visited.

William Hutchinson, 1794

William Hutchinson published his *The History of the County of Cumberland* in two volumes in 1794, printed by Francis Jollie in Carlisle. This became a standard work of reference, and describes Lorton:

> 'Arriving at Lorton, we find ourselves in the midst of a pleasant and fertile vale; the mountains opening considerably, and not so high as those to the southward. The quickset hedges are good, and the fields are regular and beautiful. Clumps of trees are here and there interspersed in the inclosures, and the skirts of the mountains are clothed with wood. The mountains here are not so awful, they bear a smoother, and more pleasing aspect. Here and there fine streams of water flow from the hills and feed the river. The yew tree delights in this situation; it is common even on the sides of the fells: in High Lorton there is one of a surprising size, spreading its branches on every side to a great distance, covering with its shade above three hundred feet in circuit. The village of Lorton is well built but the houses are too close together.'

There is no reason to doubt the size given for the High Lorton yew tree, which is, by implication, significantly larger in spread than any other in the valley.

The Wordsworths' visit in 1804

William Wordsworth in 1806 – by Edridge

William Wordsworth, amongst the many judgments of his poetic genius, has been described as a 'place-poet'. The Lake District lies at the heart of his place-poems. *Yew-trees* is one such where Lorton and Borrowdale are together in a marriage of literature, history and myth. Without this visit, such union might never have been. High Lorton would have the diminished relict of a tree with a lesser narrative. And without Wordsworth being an enterprising, indefatigable, and curious traveller; what he sees, what places tell him, his part in their dramas as actor or observer is the stuff of much of his best poetry - no Lorton poem. He began a lifetime of journeys - on foot, by cart, coach, horse-back, and boat - in 1790 to Belgium, Germany and Switzerland, North Wales, then France in 1791/2, and again, with his sister Dorothy to Germany over

1798/9, and to France in 1802; to Scotland in 1803, a long Continental tour in 1820 and in 1823; Ireland in 1829, Scotland again in 1831, and in 1837 Italy. This is no stay-at-home reclusive Cumberland gentleman. Moreover, this 'A' list omits the happy years for poetry in Dorset and Somerset with Coleridge, frequent visits to family and friends, to London, and to his 'familiar river' the 'majestic Duddon' in its winding valley. That place's particular nature and geography inspired 34 sonnets, of which the first was composed in 1806. The Duddon was the destination of the tour undertaken with Dorothy, planned, one surmises, in mid-September 1804, when Wordsworth's daughter, Dorothy (Dora), was just a month old. A good time for a break from the crowded domesticity of Dove Cottage. So, using the jaunting-car 'of the kind that is jestingly called an Irish vis-à-vis', one aged horse in the shafts, William on the dickey, Dorothy behind, seated facing outwards with the luggage at her back, they are off to the

Dorothy Wordsworth by an unknown artist, c. 1806

Duddon, via Keswick, the Whinlatter Pass and Lorton; thence along Loweswater, to Lamplugh, Ennerdale, over Cold Kell, Wasdale, Eskdale, and Seathwaite, and back to Town End. What a long way round from Grasmere - a journey of six days in an open car! Certainly the wrong way round if the Duddon was the tour's sole purpose. Why? It can only be, as Dorothy writes in her letter from Grasmere dated 7th and 10th October to Lady Beaumont - now the baby Dorothy's godmother - to visit the 'Patriarch of Yew trees'. Imagine it is the mid-afternoon on a late September day. The 'car' rattles down Tenters Lane, and turns left. The travellers are some 50 yards away from the yew tree on the beckside in its umbrageous majesty commanding the landscape. No village hall, as today, to divert the eye, only the great tree and Lorton Vale reaching, lush and green, to the fells behind; so remarkable, that William Hutchinson mentions it in his 1794 *History of Cumberland*. And this is Dorothy in a typically lively letter, here she is - as elsewhere in her journals and marvellous letters - the sensitive recorder of the 'visible world'.

> 'We seized the first fine autumnal days (my brother and I) after her recovery and took our Car to Keswick with an intention of proceeding immediately to Ennerdale and Wasdale, but the Southeys and Mrs Coleridge and Mrs Lovel went with us to Buttermere and we returned to Keswick. The next day William and I set off on our tour. We passed over the mountains of Whinlatter along the Cockermouth Road, and through the Vale of Lorton and by Loweswater to Ennerdale ... We dropped down soon after into the fertile Vale of Lorton, and went to visit a Yew tree which is the Patriarch of Yew trees, green and flourishing, in very old age – the largest tree I ever saw. We have many large ones in this Country, but I have never seen one that would not be but a branch of this. When you come we must take you to it.'

How long they stayed and looked; what resonances sounded in Wordsworth's mind as his imaginative powers dreamed into this place, we do not know. The beginning of a perception about this tree that only a poem would capture? Or confirmation of something already stirring - wherever poems come from - the re-awakening of pre-existing knowledge both of the Lorton and the Borrowdale yews? This is the significance of the visit.

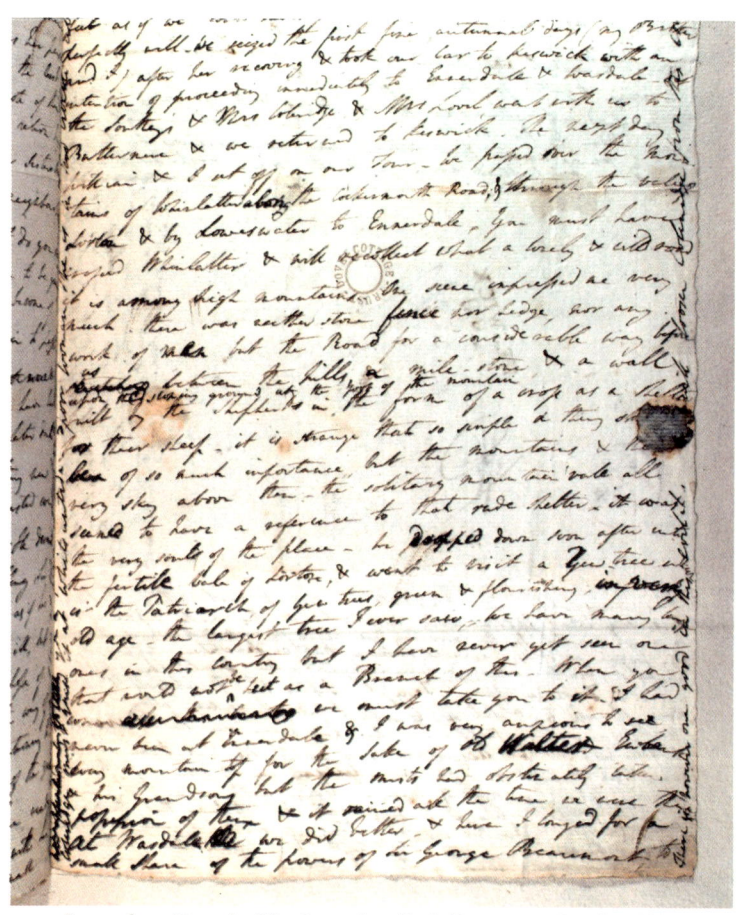

Letter from Dorothy Wordsworth to Lady Beaumont, October 1804
Courtesy of the Wordsworth Trust

The poem

The long road to the Duddon had been chosen so as to visit, en route, 'the largest tree I ever saw'. After the October letter was written, Dorothy, on known form, would have read or shown it to William before handing it on to the horse-postman to take to Keswick for the rudimentary but efficient post office - cost eight pence - for onward delivery to Lady Beamont in Dunmow, Essex. Whether it was the first sighting for brother as well as sister we do not know. The apocryphal anecdote about schoolboy William tumbling into the beck is maybe just that - a yarn. Wordsworth and Coleridge made a grand tour on foot in November 1799, including walking alongside the Cocker to Crummock. They could have stopped in Lorton. Coleridge wrote lengthy and colourful notes of the journey in his Notebooks. Nothing about the tree. So the encounter in late September 1804 may be the first. This stop on an otherwise unnecessarily devious journey, Dorothy's record for posterity in the letter to Lady Beaumont, the passage on yew trees * in her journal of the tour of Scotland, all tend to suggest that the visit is the catalyst for bringing together different strands of the creative process. The 1798 poem in *Lyrical Ballads*, the Esthwaite-sited *Lines; Left upon a Seat in a Yew-tree*, the importance of trees to Wordsworth in his real and imagined universe, the singularity and antiquity of yew trees, and much else, point to the poem being neither written nor composed in 1803. That year is associated with it for one reason only, as explained later.

* 'Having promised us sight of the largest and oldest yew-tree ever seen, she conducted us to it; it was a goodly tree, but a mere dwarf compared with several of our own country, not to speak of the giant of Lorton.'

YEW-TREES - as published in 1815

THERE is a Yew-tree, pride of Lorton Vale,
Which to this day stands single, in the midst
Of its own darkness, as it stood of yore,
Not loth to furnish weapons for the Bands
Of Umfraville or Percy ere they marched
To Scotland's Heaths; or Those that crossed the Sea
And drew their sounding bows at Azincour,
Perhaps at earlier Crecy, or Poictiers.
Of vast circumference and gloom profound
This solitary Tree!—a living thing
Produced too slowly ever to decay;
Of form and aspect too magnificent
To be destroyed. But worthier still of note
Are those fraternal Four of Borrowdale,
Joined in one solemn and capacious grove;
Huge trunks!—and each particular trunk a growth
Of intertwisted fibres serpentine
Up-coiling, and inveterately convolved,—
Nor uniformed with Phantasy, and looks
That threaten the prophane;—a pillared shade,
Upon whose grassless floor of red-brown hue,
By sheddings from the pining umbrage tinged
Perennially—beneath whose sable roof
Of boughs, as if for festal purpose, decked
With unrejoicing berries, ghostly Shapes
May meet at noontide—Fear and trembling Hope,
Silence and Foresight—Death the Skeleton
And Time the Shadow,—there to celebrate,
As in a natural temple scattered o'er
With altars undisturbed of mossy stone,
United worship; or in mute repose
To lie, and listen to the mountain flood
Murmuring from Glaramara's inmost caves.

Wordsworth dictated the following recollection to Isabella Fenwick in notes of 1843, amongst many others of his poems. Perhaps he confused 1803 with 1804. Or he had the idea of a poem drifting in his mind from the time of the tour of Scotland. The true poetic sensibility never rests.

> 'The *Yew-trees*. Grasmere 1803. These Yew-trees are still standing, but the spread of that at Lorton is much diminished by mutilation.'

In the archive of the Wordsworth Trust are four manuscript drafts of the poem. Expert opinion is that these manuscripts date much later than 1803. They bear no dates save one is dated 1803. But who wrote the date and when is unknown. If anything, that might be for the imagined composition, not its committal to paper. The dated draft might have been prepared in 1832 shortly before a four volume Poetical Works was published. The poem printed as one of the 'Poems of the Imagination' in the 1815 collection has no date. The draft overleaf starts with the line, 'that vast eugh-tree pride of Lorton Vale' and continues as in the final version. 'Eugh-tree', from the Celtic 'iw', was then an obsolete spelling, or was about to be, but had been used by Shakespeare and Edmund Spenser. The opening statement of the visible yew tree is in every draft. It fixes the voice for the consequential patriotic excursion into Border and English history. Is the space between the three lines and the leap into the Borrowdale lines significant? It would be satisfying if these are the first words of the primal draft, written in the aftermath of a September afternoon, but that is most improbable. The three other drafts, although with corrections, shew no such hesitancy.

The present assumption from available evidence is that the poem from its style and content may have been started in 1804 or 1805, and worked on, in the Wordsworth manner, between then and 1811.

— That vast eighth-wonder pride of Lorton Vale
Which to this day stands single in the midst
Of its own darkness, as it stood of yore

Nor those fraternal four of Borrowdale
Joined in one solemn & capacious grove
Huge trunks, and each particular trunk a mass
Of intertwisted fibres serpentine
Upcoiling and inveterately convolved
Nor uninformed with phantasy, and looks
That threaten the profane; a pillared shade
Upon whose grassless floor of red-brown hue
By sheddings from the pining umbrage tinged
Perennially — beneath whose sable roof
Of boughs, as if for festal purpose, decked
With unrejoicing berries, ghostly shapes
May meet at noontide; Fear & trembling Hope,
Silence, and Foresight, Death the Skeleton
And Time the Shadow, — there to celebrate
As in a natural temple scattered o'er
With altars undisturbed of mossy stone
United worship, or in mute repose
To lie and listen to the mountain flood
Murmuring from Glaramara's inmost caves

A first draft?
Courtesy of the Wordsworth Trust

Another draft
Courtesy of the Wordsworth Trust

Wordsworth showed it to his diarist friend, Henry Crabb Robinson, in 1815.

'May 9th. ... Wordsworth particularly recommended to me among his Poems of the Imagination *Yew Trees* and a description of night. These, he says, are among the best for the imaginative power displayed in them. I have since read them. They are very fine, but I believe I do not understand in what their excellence consists ... It is the mere power which he is conscious of exerting in which he delights ...'

Crabb Robinson is not so disparaging in his diary note for September 16th 1816. The two of them had been walking in Eskdale. He parted from Wordsworth on Hardknott. How he got on foot from Hardknott to the Seathwaite of the Borrowdale yews in one day is a mystery, but he writes:

Sept 16th ... As I descended to the little village of Seathwaite... I saw a woman ... She directed me to the celebrated *yew trees* on the left side of the valley. They stand in a sort of grove beyond the Buttergill Force ... The trees are five or six immense yews, famous for their age, bulk and picturesque beauty. I could only admire the *natural* curiosity. Wordsworth has thrown over them the charm of a highly poetical imagination – *vide* the new edition ...'

The entry tells that the Borrowdale yews (Crabb says 'five or six' against Wordsworth's four) and the last seventeen lines of the poem so affect him as to change his mind. The same lines that Coleridge singles out for the highest praise in Chapter XXII 'The characteristic deficits of Wordsworth's poetry...' of his *Biographia Literaria* published in 1817. Like Crabb Robinson, he reads it as a new poem. For Coleridge, quoting these lines, it is for him an example 'for this poet the gift of imagination in the highest and strictest sense of the word'. John Ruskin, too, the sage of Brantwood on Coniston, was a critical reader of *Yew-trees* and wrote in *Modern Painters* of 'the real and high action of the imagination' of the poem, and says it is 'perhaps the most vigorous and solemn bit of forest landscape ever painted.'

The Coleridge-Wordsworth friendship was the most influential, and controversial, relationship of the Romantic poetry movement. It was intimate, richly productive, difficult, and ended badly. In 1803 it was holding together but under strain. Coleridge decided to leave England for his health and negotiates a Government post in Malta. Dorothy and Mary Wordsworth diligently copy a bundle of poems for Coleridge to take with him. *Yew-trees* is not one of them. Another reason for doubting an 1803 composition.

Whether or not the great trees of Borrowdale were 'worthier still of note' with their 'ghostly Shapes' and 'pillared shade' is for tree lovers to debate. Wordsworth acknowledges there a debt to Book IX of Milton's *Paradise Lost*. Perhaps he would have wanted all the great yews he had seen made immortal; the yews of his Edenic Lake Country - Lorton, Borrowdale, and Esthwaite; those he planted in the churchyard at Grasmere and the garden yew at Dove Cottage. In a way, children of an ancestor in the mythic garden where Genesis claims that human life, for better or worse, began.

Henry Crabb Robinson
From a drawing by Masquerier

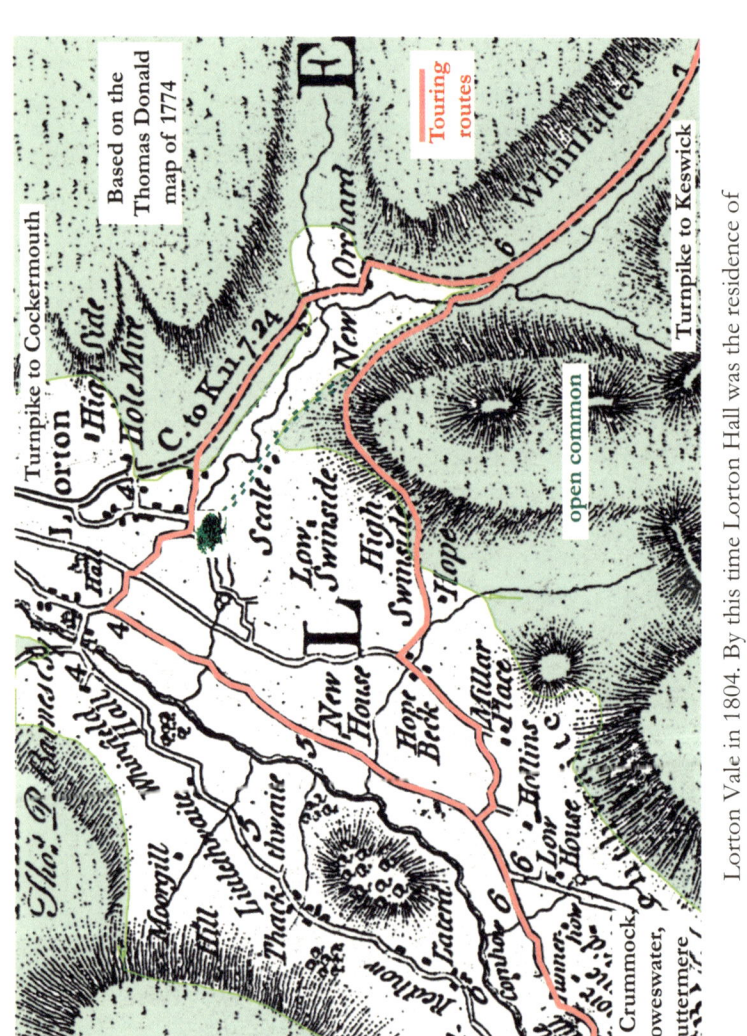

Lorton Vale in 1804. By this time Lorton Hall was the residence of Joshua Lucock (Bragg), acquaintance of the Wordsworths

The Lorton yew tree in guidebooks and histories from 1800

William Green, 1819

Guidebooks for tourists in the English lakes were published from the 1760s, including tours past Buttermere, Crummock and Loweswater, which had become more accessible after the Whinlatter Pass was turnpiked, making it suitable for carriages. However, except for Hutchinson's history already mentioned, the Lorton yew tree did not feature in a tourist guide until William Green published *The tourist's new guide* in 1819. Even Wordsworth had not included the tree in the text he wrote to accompany Rev. Joseph Wilkinson's *Select views of Cumberland, Westmoreland and Lancashire* of 1810, words that were later to become the core of Wordsworth's own guide, and his best selling book.

William Green
From H D Rawnsley, *By fell and dale*

Crummock and Buttermere, by William Green

William Green was forty when he moved to Ambleside in 1800 to earn his living as a Lakeland artist. He was a skilled draughtsman with an eye for detail and accuracy. He painted many of the natural subjects about which Wordsworth wrote, and was thought to have informed much of Wordsworth's views about landscape. After many years of friendship, Wordsworth wrote the inscription for Green's memorial at Grasmere in 1823. Like Wordsworth, he walked great distances and made a sketching tour through Lorton in July 1804, just three months before Wordsworth. His picture of Crummock and Buttermere perhaps originates from that tour, but for the yew tree in his portfolio he chose another famous yew tree in Patterdale, developing that subject in October 1804 for his portfolio at the very time that Dorothy Wordsworth was writing about the Lorton yew tree.

In his guide, which makes no reference to the poet or his works, Green identifies a number of famous yew trees:

'Yew Tree in Coniston ...
It is scarcely a mile from Shepherd's Bridge to the Yew Tree, a few houses so called as being near the famous Yew Tree, which is tall and beautiful, but not umbrageous like those of Patterdale and Lorton ...

On the Seat Oller side of the river, a short way beyond Seathwaite Bridge, stand four enormous yew trees apparently in the highest state of preservation ... The trunk of one of them is seven yards in circumference ...'

These four are, of course, the fraternal four of the poem. The Lorton tree could not be fraternal, being female, but was an inch and a half short of eight yards in circumference at that time. Green uses the famous yew tree as a landmark on the 'circuitous road' from Whinlatter, through the Vale to Scale Hill, the resting place for all 'pilgrims of taste':

The Borrowdale Yews at Evening, by A Heaton Cooper

'Scarcely a quarter of a mile past the sixth milestone, a road branches from the one to Cockermouth, and it is that, which pilgrims of taste, on foot, or horseback, and even in their carriages, pass, on their way to see Crummock Water, Low's Water, and Buttermere. Though this road along Swinside, is neither wide, nor well made on its leaving the public road, nor encouraging in scenic indications, yet, having passed the bridge, and ascended the hill, its explorer is charmed with a sudden and extraordinary change …

The road from Keswick to Whitehaven has been noticed to the sixth milestone, which stands on Whinlatter, halfway between Keswick and Cockermouth. A few hundred yards beyond this stone, is the deviating road by Swinside to Scale Hill. Though on passing from Keswick to Cockermouth the first half is superior to the latter, the latter half has many charming features. A rumbling stream, deeply engulphed in rocks and wood, is the traveller's companion all the way to the foot of the hill. Below New Orchard, on this descent, the Italian looking bridge crossing a gully, deserves the artist's attention. The higher end of Lorton is gradually unfolded to the spectator on his nearing **the famous yew tree**, eight miles from Keswick. Here the circuitous road to Scale Hill leaves the turnpike road…'

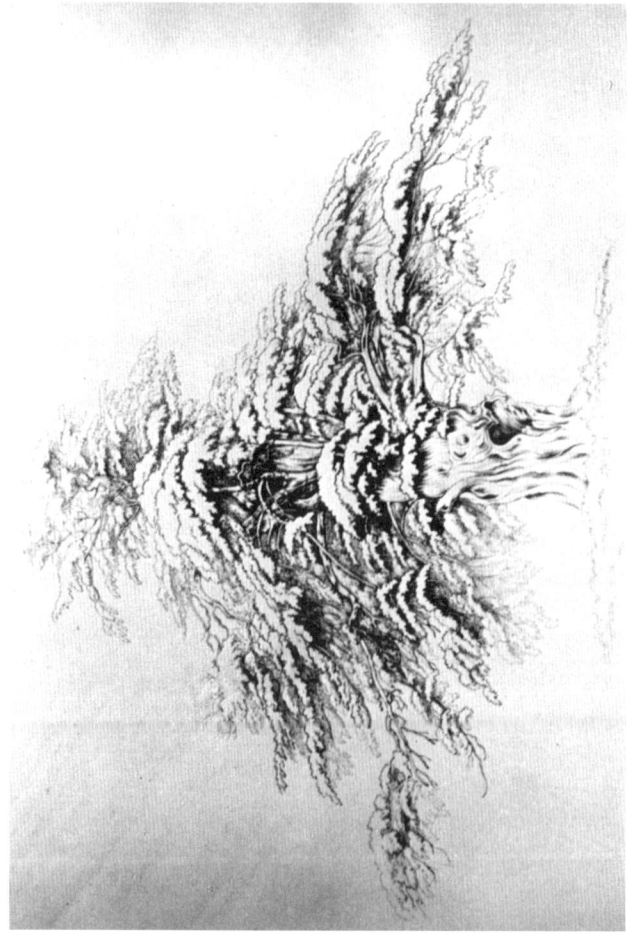

Yew tree at Patterdale, by William Green, 1804

'Black's picturesque guide to the English Lakes' from 1841

It was not until 1841 that the celebrity of the elderly Wordsworth and his poetry were used to embellish guides to the lakes. Black's guide, with various editors, was the first to link the yew trees at Borrowdale and Lorton with the poem:

> 'In the vicinity of the lead mine are four yews of extraordinary size. Wordsworth, having mentioned the large yew which is "the pride of Lorton vale" commemorates these trees ...' (poem extract follows)

> 'From Scale Hill the tourist may proceed to Cockermouth, ... or return to Keswick by the vale of Lorton, a distance of twelve miles ... Four miles from Scale Hill the Keswick and Cockermouth road is entered, near the Yew-tree which Wordsworth has celebrated ...' (poem extract follows)

The editor of Black's guide in 1843, Phillips, did not share Wordsworth's optimism for the future, and soon after the following words were published, the Lorton yew tree was hit by the fateful storm:

> 'There are some fine remains of the yew extant in the lake country, witness the Lorton, Borrowdale, and Patterdale Trees noticed in this volume. Some of the limestone escarpments have numbers climbing up their sides; but, in consequence of their exposed situation they are but poor specimens of a tree which, when enormous bulk is joined, as sometimes happens, to the venerableness of antiquity, presents one of the most striking objects in the vegetable creation ... Since the introduction of fire-arms, the cultivation of the yew has been altogether neglected: but when we consider that it furnished our ancestors with their most valued weapons and that its

connexion in this way with Agincourt, with Cressy, and other well-fought fields, is a noticeable and brilliant fact in our history, some little attention should, we think, be directed to its encouragement, although it has long ceased to be a *useful* tree. It is to be feared that its extinction, except as a garden curiosity, will otherwise soon be complete.

> "The warlike Yew, with which, more than the lance,
> The strong arm'd English spirits conquer'd France."
>   WILLIAM BROWNE'

'A complete guide to the lakes'
John Hudson, 1842

This work, edited by John Hudson in 1842, included Mr Wordsworth's guide to the scenery. The tour through Lorton is derived from Green's description but links the tree to the poem extract via the asterisk in the text:

> 'The more circuitous route through the Vale of Lorton turns off from the Cockermouth road at the famous Yew Tree* and joins the terrace road just noticed above a mile and a half from Scale Hill.'

'A complete guide to the English lakes'
Harriet Martineau, 1855

Harriet Martineau in 1849, by George Richmond

Harriet Martineau descended on Ambleside society like a whirlwind in 1845 and soon built her own house. She was already a leading female writer, and became a friend of the ageing Wordsworth, though, as he wrote to Henry Crabb Robinson, she was 'in many respects ... a dangerous companion'. Her guide, *A complete guide to the English lakes*, was first published in 1855, five years after the poet's death. It included the yew tree *en passant* as she took the Swinside terrace route from Scale Hill:

> 'The turn is to the right, at about a mile from Scale Hill, leaving the Cockermouth road, which traverses the vale of Lorton. The higher he ascends, the more lovely are the views over that vale that the traveller obtains, till at length the Solway gleams in the sun, and the Scotch mountains appear beyond. If he has good eyes, the driver will point out to him, at a vast distance, **the famous old Lorton yew** appearing like a dark clump, beside a white farmhouse. When fairly under Whinlatter, six or seven miles from Scale Hill, he cannot but admire, — in one or the other sense of the word, — the colouring of the hill itself, if the time be anywhere from June to September. The gaudy hues of the mingled gorse and heather are, at that season, unlike any exhibition of colour we have seen elsewhere, — exceeding even the far-famed American forest. As the north-western vision vanishes, the south-eastern opens; and the vale of Keswick and Skiddaw in its noblest aspect and the lakes far below, looks finer than ever. After passing through Braithwaite, he soon recognises the road, and returns to Keswick by the well-known bridge over the Derwent.'

'Guide to Cockermouth'
John Askew, 1866

Askew takes a circular tour from Cockermouth and approaches Lorton from Whinfell over the bridge:

> 'On leaving this place, the first turn on the left leads over Lorton Bridge into the village of Low Lorton. Proceeding direct for about a quarter of a mile, we come to the famous Lorton Yew, a tree immortalised by Wordsworth in undying song, and by George Fox for having sheltered his friend James Lancaster in the year 1652, whilst he was preaching to an immense concourse of people. Fox writes (page 201 of his Journal):- "This tree was so full of people that I feared they would break it down." A guard of Cromwell's soldiers, twelve in number, who happened to be stationed at Lorton during that time, kept the meeting in order. The evening shadow of this tree, when in its prime, covered an acre of ground. About twenty years ago a part of it was blown down, and the owner contemplated its entire removal, but the strong protests of some influential friends led him to desist from his purpose. From the great thickness of the trunk its estimated age is about one thousand years.'

The Wordsworth scholar, the artist and the Whinfell Quaker 1878-1887

Professor William Knight played a key role in early Wordsworth scholarship, and in 1878 he published *The English lake district as interpreted by the poems of Wordsworth*, the first guide to give primacy to Wordsworth's poetry. He prints the poem in full, noting that 'the "pride of Lorton vale" referred to at the beginning of this poem, still survives, majestic in decay'. In the 1904 edition he gives an account of the damage to the Borrowdale grove in 1883. His purpose, in part at least, was to record the geography of the poetical works:

> 'Many of Wordsworth's allusions to Place are obscure: and the exact localities, as well as individual objects, are difficult to identify. It is doubtful if he cared whether they could be afterwards traced out or not.'

Following the 1878 publication, two readers made important responses, which were to engender a second book. Firstly, Harry Goodwin, the artist, visited the sites given by Knight as the 'places' of the poems, making sketches of the locations, which he inserted in the pages and sent to Professor Knight. Secondly, Wilson Robinson of Whinfell Hall, a Quaker landowner, wrote to Professor Knight in 1880 giving an account of the tree since the 1820s, when as a young man he measured its girth. This Wilson Robinson was the father of the well-known climber, John Wilson Robinson, but the father was also a climber; the first person known to sketch Napes Needle, in 1828.

The pride of Lorton Vale, by Harry Goodwin, about 1880

In 1887, Goodwin and Knight published *Through the Wordsworth Country*, in which the sketches were each accompanied by Knight's letterpress. From this book we have the text of Wilson Robinson's account and the first surviving sketch of the Lorton yew tree, though after the destruction described by Robinson:

> 'THIS Lorton Yew is described in the poem attached to the preceding drawing of the Borrowdale Grove. It is greatly reduced in size and majesty since Wordsworth wrote his poem, and is now very much of a ruin. Mr. Wilson Robinson, of Whinfell Hall, Cockermouth, wrote to me of it thus in May, 1880:
> "The tree in outline expanded towards the root considerably; then, at about two feet from the ground, the trunk began to separate into huge limbs, spreading in all directions. I once measured this trunk at its least circumference, and found it 23 feet 10 inches. For the last fifty or sixty years the branches have been gradually dying on the south-east side, and about twenty-five years ago a strong south-east gale, coming with accumulated force down Hope Gill, and - owing to the tree being so open on that side - taking it laterally at a disadvantage, wrenched off one of the great side branches down to the ground, carrying away nearly a third of the tree. This event led to further peril; for, the second portion having been sold to a cabinet-maker at Whitehaven for £15 this gave the impression that the wood was valuable (owing to the celebrity of the tree); and a local wood-monger bought the remainder. Two men worked half a day to grub it up; but a Cockermouth medical gentleman, hearing what was going on, made representations to the owner, and it ended in the woodmen sparing the remainder of the tree, which was not much the worse for what had been done. Many large dead branches have also been cut off, and now we have to regret that the pride of Lorton Vale, shorn of its ancient dignity, is but a ruin, much more venerable than picturesque." '

John Bolton, the lecture of 1891

A native of Cockermouth, John Bolton, 1855-1915, was a keen student of local customs and dialect, wrote poetry published in the West Cumberland Times, and became the first true local historian of Cockermouth and Lorton Vale. After Cheltenham College, he was appointed master at Lorton School where he served from 1877 to 1882. Afterwards he returned to Cockermouth to the family building business. In 1891 he gave a lecture on Lorton and Loweswater, and their inhabitants, in the period around 1811 when his mother-in-law, Mrs Lancaster, born 1802 in Brackenthwaite, was a young girl.

> 'The person who held Boon Beck farm before Peter Iredale took it was a man named Brown who left Boon Beck for his own place at Bassenthwaite. Before that Porter White was the tenant and here was born in 1794 his son Joseph and another son was Ballantyne White. This Porter White was the grandfather of Joseph White of "White and Stoddart" Cockermouth. When Mrs Lancaster's father took the farm, farm produce was extremely dear on account of the war with France, and the rent was consequently dear. After the close of the war 1815 things came down, but the country was in a very bad state. While they were at Boonbeck the barn and threshing machine and sheds were built and the race water wheel made...
> The man who did this work was Gilbert Sowerby of Cockermouth. The Yew Tree was a very big tree then but Mr. Stubbs cut down a great many large limbs and sold it to make weaver's shuttles. What would Wordsworth have thought if he had known the tree he wrote about was cut down to make Weaver's shuttles? ... I believe Miss Sim had some furniture made out of a portion of it and Mr. Grayson has in his possession some furniture made from it.'

The Mr. Stubbs mentioned above was Robert Stubbs, whose family had held Boonbeck Farm for centuries.

John Bolton's best-known work was a history of Cockermouth, *Wordsworth's Birthplace,* published in 1912, in which he gives a version of the George Fox narrative, firmly placed in Lorton. But his greatest contribution to the lore of the Lorton yew tree was to write a poem, published in the West Cumberland Times.

THE LORTON YEW

Here by the stream it stands alone,
  As verdant and as hale
As when the Britons' bows were draw
  To guard this lovely vale.
It stands the pride of Lorton still.
  Although its glory's done,
For centuries its seen yon hill
  Reflect the ev'ning sun.
By archers sought in bygone days
  To furnish trusty bows,
When Lorton men in bloody frays
  Defeated Scottish foes.
It grew a tree of great resort,
  And 'neath its ample shade
The villagers enjoyed their sport
  On merry May-day made.
And oft it looked on happy scenes,
  As when, beneath its bowers,
They decked the bonny village queens
  With wreaths of wildwood flowers.
Long may it stand, a link to bind
  Us to the jocund past—
But, Ah, the sport of time and wind
  'Twill die and fall at last.

'Literary associations of the lake district'
Canon H D Rawnsley, 1894

Rawnsley's writing combines religion, poetry and scenery into a seamless whole, with Fox and Wordsworth invoked and enjoined with the author, seeming to travel together through the locations with a common purpose. Rawnsley is not too troubled with historical accuracy, having a higher purpose in mind, but the high quality and force of his prose defy the reader to question the detail. 'For Fox's and for Wordsworth's sake, one could wish that no railway had ruined the original site of the latter well' ... (i.e. the Nun's Well at Brigham, desecrated by the Workington and Cockermouth Railway in 1848). In *Literary Associations* he speaks briefly of the 'majesty of the Lorton Yew' but his pen is saved for the later essay, 'A famous yew-tree' in his *Lake Country Sketches* of 1903, almost at the centenary of the Wordsworth visit. This we print in full and in facsimile from page 55, having no hope of equalling Rawnsley's work. There seems no doubt that George Fox would have been reconciled to the Anglican communion.

In 1896 Rawnsley also conceived, promoted and edited a small book, *A Reminiscence of Wordsworth Day*. This marks the unveiling of the memorial fountain, pictured overleaf in Harris Park, Cockermouth, to the memory of William and Dorothy Wordsworth, April 7th, 1896.

The memorial fountain, Harris Park, Cockermouth, 1896

'Two thousand miles of wanderings in the border country, Lakeland and Ribblesdale;' Edmund Bogg, 1898

Edmund Bogg provides a most comprehensive and detailed combination of travel, history and literature based on the personal experience of many years. He describes both Lorton and the yew tree:

> 'Midway in the vale stands the village of Lorton, composed of one long narrow street of whitewashed houses with overhanging eaves; there is a primitive and old-world aspect about the place. It was here we met an aged man who had seen ninety-three winters, and had conversed with William Wordsworth before he had reached middle life, and who spoke of the poet familiarly as "William". The old man was fairly erect, and, considering his ninety-three years, in good health. I met him taking his afternoon walk, nearly a mile from his home ...
>
> The old Yew tree described by Wordsworth is at High Lorton, but is now only a wreck of its former glory. It stands in the corner of a field fenced off for protection by railings.'

Bogg includes numerous drawings and photographs in his wanderings, the sketch of the yew tree being by A Haselgrave.

The pride of Lorton vale, by A Haselgrave in Bogg, 1898

'The English Lakes'
Frederick Brabant, 1902

The sad duty of reporting the demise of the Lorton yew tree fell to Frederick Gashard Brabant in Methuen's little guide series, where under Lorton he reports:

> 'Its yew tree, celebrated by Wordsworth, is no longer in existence, having shared the fate of the tree which gave its name to Yewdale, and which is rapidly overtaking the Yews of Borrowdale'.

How Brabant discovered this information is unknown, but one suspects that he did not make a personal survey, which might have led him to a different conclusion. But his report helped to confuse matters and to lead subsequent twentieth century writers to believe that the tree was variously destroyed, lost, rediscovered, elsewhere, or mythical.

But it is clear that the famous Lorton yew tree remained, and still remains, where it has been for a millennium.

The Lorton yew-tree, date and photographer unknown
Courtesy of Ted Petty

The life of the Lorton yew tree

From the evidence of the records it is possible to reconstruct the life of the tree and to establish its size and setting when the Wordsworths visited. Is the poem accurately descriptive, or exaggerated, as the present tree suggests; its current girth indicating a mere 600-800 year age?

From Wilson Robinson's 1820s measurement we know that it is likely to be 1100-1400 years old, about as old as Lorton. From Hutchinson we know that, in 1794, the tree was special among many, and that its spread was about 20 metres, right across the beck, almost to the road. William Green called it umbrageous, in that it was remarkable for its spread, not its height. John Askew claimed that its evening shadow covered an acre of ground. Wilson Robinson speaks of huge limbs, starting two feet from the ground and spreading in all directions. These, then, were suitable seats for the audience for James Lancaster, not George Fox, in 1653.

And the setting? In 1800 there was no brewery, no brewery cottages, no malt house (now the Yew Tree Hall), no Yew Tree View cottages and no Corner House until 1809, when built by William Jennings, who had malt kilns by the beck. Only Boonbeck farm stood nearby. On its strategic site the yew tree imposed itself on the five wall-free roads which approached the tree, unobscured and dominant. That it was known as one of a group of famous yew trees is attested by Green, Black, Martineau and Rawnsley.

There were taller trees and older trees, but in its solitary position, it would seem to justify Dorothy Wordsworth's descriptions as 'the giant of Lorton', and the 'Patriarch of Yew-trees'. Likewise it can be seen that Wordsworth's descriptors 'solitary in the midst of its own darkness' and of 'vast circumference and gloom profound' were, typically, an accurate description of nature from which to start a journey of imagination.

Then came the destruction, mostly the work of nature. Wilson Robinson reported south-east limbs dying off from the 1820s or 1830s and Bolton reports that Mr Stubbs cut down a number of limbs for weavers' shuttles. This is probably the mutilation regretted by Wordsworth in 1843, but surely Mr Stubbs would have used only those dying limbs? The storm that removed a third of the tree would have occurred in the 1850s. After another third was sold, the third that was saved from destruction became the basis of the tree today, the giant less its limbs and two thirds of its trunk. Rawnsley reports a further large loss, but his photograph shows another huge limb, which must have been lost in the twentieth century, long before the storm of 1999. The tree has been protected from the attentions of man since 1949, when Cumberland County Council issued a preservation order; but the wind is the main enemy, and does not read preservation orders. At least there is comfort in knowing that, although the tree is much smaller than before, a smaller tree can better withstand future storms.

Photographs for the Bicentenary
by David Herrod

A poem for the bicentenary
by Jacob Polley

The Yew

Out of the dark, as old as the cold,
the yew comes to stand beside a millstream.
The archers who might have stripped its bark
are dead, the cabinet-makers have gone:
empires withered while the yew grew on.

It's been struck by lightning and lives,
kills cattle that nibble it, cools hencoops;
has changed less than languages, calendars,
coins; has watched gods wash away in the rain.

Ever twisted, folded, evergreen –
its trunk flakes, its branches scrape the ground:
in its shade, nothing grows,
but the rinds of its edible berries glow.

The Lorton yew tree, from *Meetings with remarkable trees, 1994*
Courtesy of Thomas Pakenham

The common yew; taxus baccata
John Spedding
President, Royal Society of Forestry

The common yew occupies a singular position amongst our native British trees. Yew trees feature in various guises in many parts of our landscape. This booklet will help to underline the worth of these trees as individual characters.

Yew trees are either male or female. The male flowers produce a mass of pollen in February. Female trees have small green flowers, which, by September, turn red with a cavity holding the seed. The leaves, seeds, bark and wood are all toxic.

The trees grow slowly. A young tree may add 8 - 12 inches in height and half an inch in girth yearly. Old trees no longer increase their height. They may add less than 0.2 of an inch in girth each year.

The yew lives to a great age. Many are over 1,000 years old and a few over 2,000 years. This achievement is partly due to its being comparatively wind-firm, whilst its dense, poisonous wood hosts only two common parasites (an oak tree may host up to two hundred or more). Also, when a yew loses a limb, new shoots grow to protect injured areas of the tree. Many yews are hollow, but the wood is still sufficiently robust to uphold the branch system.

Yews often derive from wind-blown seed. Those that have been planted have been so for various reasons. They may afford shelter to wells, gardens or cottages. Many have been grown for ornament as topiary or hedges. Others have been planted to mark a boundary or a meeting place for a Hundred Court. Perhaps the most likely place to find a yew is in the local churchyard. Many possible reasons for such a planting have been advanced. These include, to symbolise eternal life, to mark a place of sanctuary or to keep a graveyard clean by the shade of the trees. Frequently yews, now in churchyards, predate the Christian era and may have been associated with earlier religions.

In prehistoric times, spears were often made from yew wood. Later, longbows were made from it, but, in the middle ages, the wood for the English longbow more often came from Spain. In more recent times, yew wood has been used by furniture makers and wood turners. Presently, young foliage is used for making Paclitaxel, a cancer treatment drug.

In many parts of Britain, place names include reference to the yew, for example, in Cumbria, there is Yew How, reputed to be a Norse burial ground, on the slopes of Latrigg near Keswick. Ivegill, near Carlisle, is the valley of the river *Ive*, an old Scandinavian name for *Yew*.

These are times in which, happily, we have come to afford to veteran trees the respect and care which they deserve. The Lorton Yew, with its nineteen foot girth, is a venerable example of this distinguished tree. It is satisfying to know that it is now being celebrated in the way of which, doubtless, William Wordsworth would have approved.

As President of the Royal Forestry Society and a Fellow of the Wordsworth Trust, I find that two of my close interests converge in this key feature of the Vale of Lorton. And so it gives me particular pleasure to make a contribution to this booklet.

The Lorton yew tree, from *The Cumbrian yew book, 1999*
Courtesy of Ken Mills

The Lorton yew, Canon Rawnsley, 1903

'A famous yew-tree'
by Canon H D Rawnsley

A facsimile from 'Lake country sketches', 1903

A FAMOUS YEW-TREE.

THERE is a passage in George Fox's *Journal* that brings one face to face with a brave man of God, reveals the spirit of true martyrdom, and makes one envious of his dazzling courage:
'Now were great threatenings given forth in Cumberland that if ever I came there again they would take away my life. When I heard it, I was drawn to go to Cumberland, and went to the same parish whence these threatenings came, but they had not power to touch me.'

It is a passage that attracts one to the apostle of the leathern-apron, and makes one desire to know the scenes of his life's travail. It was not to be wondered at, therefore, that when one found oneself at Keswick in a neighbouring valley to Lorton, one should wish to visit one of the places ever associated with his memory, and see the spot whence

55

A FAMOUS YEW-TREE

the echoes of the preacher's voice have never died.

Associated with this wish to follow the footsteps of George Fox, was the desire to see the Yew-tree, 'Pride of Lorton Vale,' which, on the day of Fox's sermon, provided seats for the listeners. For the famous yew-trees in the Lake District are becoming each year fewer. It is true that the great yew in Tilberthwaite is still standing, but that famous hollow trunk that kept alive the name of the mission preacher St. Patrick, in Patrick's Dale or Patterdale, has fallen; and the great winter storm of 1883 worked havoc upon Seathwaite's sacred brotherhood:

> 'Those fraternal four of Borrowdale,
> Joined in one solemn and capacious grove;
> Huge trunks!—and each particular trunk a growth
> Of intertwisted fibres serpentine
> Up-coiling and inveterately convolved—'

are now a wreck,—one fell, the others were riven to pieces.

Here in the Lake District, by command of bluff King Hal, each estatesman was obliged to plant a yew-tree by his homestead, in order that he might never lack of wood for his bow when he was called—as he not unfrequently was called—to the Marches, in defence of the

Border. And in many places, long after the homestead has passed away, the solitary yew survives to tell us of the troublous times of old. It was not long since an estatesman sent down to the local museum of Keswick the old oaken bow-chest of his fathers, which, though it has been long used as a meal-ark, by its carving clearly shows it was intended for other use. The family name of Bowman is a common one in Cumberland, and still in our neighbourhood the field-names preserve a memory of the village bowman's prowess, and the 'butts' field is a word of common parlance.

But it is George Fox, the man of peace, that we were most interested in, as we crossed the Keswick Valley and climbed the long slope of Whinlatter to pay a visit to the brave man's preaching place, and it was mere coincidence that that preaching place should be associated with weapons of war.

People do not realise how fair a view of the whole Skiddaw range is presented to them as they climb that pass, or they would climb it oftener. The higher one climbs, the higher does Skiddaw appear, and deep-bosomed mountain-side in all its massy grandeur of emerald green and lilac shade in spring, of puce and burnished bronze in autumn, impresses one with its calm and restfulness. The cloud, sure sign of fine weather, rests upon its utmost peak to-day, and irresistibly recalls the lines of Wordsworth's sonnet:

'Veiling itself in mid-Atlantic clouds
To pour forth streams more sweet than Castaly,'

while the pleasant farms with the far-off interchange of happy cock-crowing, glitter at our feet, and, like an arm of some great ocean-loch, the white waters of Bassenthwaite come round the precipice of Barf, and sweep out of the shadow of Wythop woods into the September sunshine. On our left rises Grasmoor, haunt of the dottrel, and Hobcarton Crag, beloved of rare mountain flowers. So we crest the long slope and drop down into Lorton, with the hill-sides on our right, golden with gorse against the westering sun. Turning sharply to the left as soon as the village is reached, we pass a kind of pleasant rural street, if that may be called a street which has houses only on the one side of it, and just as we emerge into the country again, find ourself at a spot where the road forks, a portion of it going over a beck bridge into a farm enclosure by a picturesque old water-mill and byre, and a portion of it,—the main road to Loweswater,—bending sharply to the right to go across the valley by the north side of the stream, which is here hidden from view by a long barn building. If we pause at this point we cannot help being struck by the sombre mass of a great yew-tree standing in a pleasant meadow close to the beck, where at one time there was doubtless a ford. This is what Wordsworth described as

> 'A yew-tree, Pride of Lorton Vale,
> Which to this day stands single, in the midst
> Of its own darkness, as it stood of yore,
> Not loth to furnish weapons for the bands
> Of Umfraville or Percy ere they marched
> To Scotland's heaths; or those that crossed the sea
> And drew their sounding bows at Azincour,
> Perhaps at earlier Crecy, or Poictiers.
> Of vast circumference and gloom profound
> This solitary tree!—a living thing
> Produced too slowly ever to decay;
> Of form and aspect too magnificent
> To be destroyed.'

It is not to-day the noble tree it was when Fox was here, and the prophecy of the poet was only a few years since like to have been made utterly vain. For its form and aspect was so magnificent that its owner sold it to a Lorton wood merchant, and it was just about to be cut down when some memory of Fox's

A FAMOUS YEW-TREE

sermon awoke in the breast of a faithful member of the Society of Friends in the neighbourhood, and the wood merchant good-naturedly went off his bargain.

It is true that it shows no signs of decay, but it has suffered loss. Two of its main stems were shattered years ago by a hurricane, and were sawn off at the bole. Let us go along the road to the farm buildings, and turn back down to what now serves for a watering-place for horses. It is thus we shall best get an idea of how 'it stands single, in the midst of its own darkness.'

The branches stretch their shadow over the stream, and the ripple of the sunny talkative beck contrasts strangely with the deep silence of the solemn tree. If we go up to Whinfell Hall and ask a keen observer of nature and plant life about this famous yew, Mr. Wilson Robinson will tell us that he once measured the trunk at its least circumference and found it 23 feet 10 inches, and that, about thirty years ago, a strong southeast gale came with hurricane force down Hope Ghyll, wrenched off one of the side limbs and carried away a third of the tree. Another limb has fallen since then, and yet, shattered and torn, what a magnificent ruin it is, how well worth climbing over Whinlatter Pass to visit.

After gazing up the beck towards the picturesque bridge from which we first surveyed the yew, towards the grand old farmstead and its cluster of sycamores as a background for the bridge, let us go back to the bridge and across into the meadow wherein the 'Pride of Lorton Vale' stands, and, gazing from under the tree towards the west and south, let us wonder at the beauty of faintly bronzed fern on Whiteside, the amethystine lilac of the Grasmoor mass, the far-off cones of Red Pike and High Stile blue above Mellbreak, and far to the west, Herdhouse ghostly grey; all seeming to join in shutting out the world and making the quiet emerald meadow in which we stand a sanctuary for thought and restfulness.

Then let us go back to that day in the year 1653 when George Fox, having narrowly escaped death by a boy's rapier thrust, and with his hand and wrist still smarting from the cruel blow of a rough fellow down at Bootle, where they mobbed him on the previous Sunday, pale and worn came hither to the ford and found already James Lancaster, one of his disciples, who had gone forward as an avant-courier on the way to Cockermouth, busy haranguing the people.

The quiet meadow of to-day was on that day full of armed men. A detachment of Cromwell's soldiers had been told off from Cockermouth to keep the peace—it being known that Fox was on his way to Lorton; and Mr. Larkham, the Congregationalist minister of Cockermouth, and Priest Wilkinson, the Vicar of Brigham-cum-Mosser-cum-Lorton, were probably among the crowd that covered the field and stood by the banks of the stream. 'The people,' we read in Fox's *Journal*, 'lay up and down in the open, like people at a leaguer.' Fox had seen something of camp life during the late civil war, and he doubtless felt that day that, man of peace though he was, the field of the Lorton yew would be indeed a field of battle for him.

But what interests us most as we gaze upon this venerable tree to-day in these pleasant pastures beside the waters of peace, is not so much the memory of the crowd of Cromwellian soldiers and members of the Church militant who came out that day to 'sorely withstand' George Fox, as the vision of the boughs of this sable and majestic yew-tree filled with the listening ears and eager eyes of those who heard that day the weary and way-worn prophet of the Lord, 'largely declare the word of Life' as he knew it, and 'open the everlasting Gospel to them.' Fox tells us that 'this tree was so full of people that I feared they would break it down.'

Look at it now, and think of it no longer as a broken yew-tree, sown here perchance by some far wandering bird centuries ago, but as a living witness to the power of men who have a living Gospel to declare to win the souls of their fellows, and lead them into communion with God who is a spirit. Men once heard the voice of Fox sound out here, above the babble of the beck and the hum of the multitude and the protests of the Lorton minister, and those who crowded on the yew-tree boughs felt light instead of darkness—sun instead of shadow, was their portion, and we read, 'Many hundreds were convinced that day, and received the Lord Jesus Christ and His free teaching with gladness.'

We are not Quakers, but at least our hearts beat in unison with the earnest teacher of the Truth he knew, to an age that was helped and is still helped by that Truth ; and as we leave the field of the tree,

> 'Not loth to furnish weapons for the bands
> Of Umfraville or Percy ere they marched
> To Scotland's heaths; or those that crossed the sea
> And drew their sounding bows at Azincour,'

we rejoice to think that beneath its sable boughs, the preacher of the way of peace as better than war, once preached a sermon ; and we trust, that for many a long year still, 'single in the midst of its own darkness as it stood of yore,' may stand the Lorton Yew.

Contributors

David Herrod lives in Mockerkin. He is a multiple award-winning photographer with a comprehensive portfolio. His work is used commercially and collected privately, corporately and by public bodies such as the National Portrait Gallery and Victoria and Albert Museum in London. He writes for magazines and exhibits widely. He has had three books published, one being *Waters of Cumbria*, now in its second edition.

Jacob Polley was born in Carlisle in 1975, where he still lives and works. His first book, *The Brink*, (2003), was short listed for the T S Eliot Prize. He won the Arts Council of England's 'First Verse' prize in April 2002 and previously, an Eric Gregory Award from the Society of Authors.

John Spedding CBE lives at West Mirehouse near Keswick with his wife Clare. They have two married sons. He retired from practice at the Bar in 1996. He is currently President of the Royal Forestry Society. He is also a Fellow of the Wordsworth Trust and a Vice-President of the Tennyson Society.

Dr Robert Woof CBE is the Director of the Wordsworth Trust at Dove Cottage, the 'Centre for British Romanticism'. A leading Wordsworth scholar, writer and publisher, he has organised over 20 exhibitions here and abroad, conferences and literary events. In 2005 at Grasmere the Jerwood Centre opens, which will hold the Trust's collection of over 50,000 items: manuscripts, prints, drawings and paintings.

Bibliography

Askew, John. *Guide to Cockermouth.* 2nd Ed Editor Thomas Thompson, Cockermouth, Isaac Evening, 1872.
Bevan-Jones, Robert. *The Ancient Yew. A History of Taxus baccata.* Macclesfield, Windgather Press, 2002.
Bogg, Edmund. *Two thousand miles of wandering in the border country, Lakeland and Ribblesdale.* Leeds, E Bogg, 1898.
Bolton, John. *Lorton and Loweswater Eighty Years Ago.* In 'Cockermouth Miscellanea', Cumbria Family History Society, undated, original 1891.
Bolton, John. *Wordsworth's birthplace: being the parochial history and local government of the ancient borough of Cockermouth.* Cockermouth, Fletcher, 1912.
Bowers, Frederick. *Reference and Deixis in Wordsworth's 'Yew-trees'.* English Studies in Canada 5 (1979), pp 292-300.
Brabant, Frederick Gashard. *The English Lakes.* Methuen, The Little Guide Series, 1902.
Burkett, M E *William Green of Ambleside: a Lake District artist, 1760-1823.* Kendal, Abbot Hall Art Gallery, 1984.
Coleridge, Samuel Taylor. *Biographia literaria, or, Biographical sketches of my literary life and opinions.* London, Rest Fenner, 1817.
Davies, Hunter. *William Wordsworth.* Stroud, Sutton, 2003.
Donald, Thomas. *Historic map of Cumberland 1774.* CWAAS Record Series Vol XV, 2002.
Friends Historical Society. *The first publishers of Truth: being early records of the introduction of Quakerism into the counties of England and Wales.* Headley Bros, 1907.
Fox, George. *Journal of George Fox.* Cash, 1852.
Gambles, Robert. *Out of the forest - the natural world and place names of Cumbria.* Kendal, Laverock Books, 1989.
Gill, Stephen Charles. *William Wordsworth: A Life.* Oxford, Clarendon Press, New York, Oxford University Press, 1989
George, Ron. *A Cumberland Valley, A history of the parish of Lorton.* Ontario, Bovate Publications, 2003.

Green, William. *The tourist's new guide, containing a description of the lakes, mountains and scenery in Cumberland, Westmorland, and Lancashire ...* Kendal, R. Lough, 1819.
Goodwin, Harry and Knight, William Angus. *Through the Wordsworth country.* London, Swan Sonnenschein, Lowrey & Co, 1887.
Hartman, Geoffrey H. *The Use and Abuse of Structural Analysis in Riffatere's Interpretation of Wordsworth's 'Yew Trees'.* New Literary History 7 (1975), pp 165-89.
Holmes, Richard. *Coleridge: Early Visions.* London, Hodder & Stoughton, 1989.
Hudson, John G H. *A complete guide to the Lakes ... with Mr. Wordsworth's description of the scenery ... and three letters on the geology of the Lake District by Professor Sedgwick.* Kendal, J Hudson, 1843.
Hudson, John G H. *Hand-book for visitors to the English Lakes with an introduction by the late W Wordsworth Esq.* Kendal, Wilson, 1855.
Hutchinson, William. *The history of the county of Cumberland and some places adjacent ...* Carlisle, Jollie, 1794.
Jones, Enid Huws. *There is a yew tree ...* Cumbria, 1986, Dalesman Publishing, Kendal.
Knight, William Angus. *The English lake district as interpreted in the poems of Wordsworth.* Edinburgh, D Douglas, 3rd Ed, 1904.
Lindop, Grevel. *A literary guide to the Lake District.* Chatto & Windus, 1993.
Linton, E Lynn. *The lake country.* London, Smith, Elder and Co, 1864.
Martineau, Harriet. *A complete guide to the English lakes.* London, Whittaker & Co, 2nd Ed, 1860.
Mills Ken. *The Cumbrian Yew Book.* Solway Rural Initiative, 1999
Pakenham, Thomas. *Meetings with remarkable trees.* UK, Cassell, 1996.
Phillips, John. *Black's picturesque guide to the English Lakes: including the geology of the district.* Edinburgh, Black, 1846.
Rawnsley, Hardwicke Drummond. *Literary associations of the English lakes.* Glasgow, J MacLehose and Sons, 1894.
Rawnsley, Hardwicke Drummond. *Lake country sketches,* Glasgow, J MacLehose and Sons, 1903.
Reed, Mark L. *Wordsworth: the chronology of the middle years, 1800-1815.* Cambridge, Mass, Harvard University Press, 1975.
Riffaterre, Michael. *Interpretation and Descriptive poetry: A Reading of Wordsworth's 'Yew-Trees'.* New Literary History 4 (1973), pp 229-56.

Robinson, Henry Crabb. *Henry Crabb Robinson on books and their writers.* Dent, 1928.

Rouff, Gene W. *Wordsworth's 'Yew-trees' and romantic perception.* Modern language Quarterly 34 (1973), pp 146-60.

Ruskin, John. *Modern Painters.* London, Smith Elder, 1843. Vol II, Pt III, Sec IV, Ch IV, p214.

Twitchell, James B. *Romantic Horizons: Aspects of the Sublime in English Poetry and Painting, 1770-1850.* Columbia, University of Missouri, 1983.

Wilkinson, Joseph. *Select Views in Cumberland, Westmoreland and Lancashire.* Ackermann, 1810.

Woof, Pamela. *Reading Paradise Lost.* The Wordsworth Trust, Grasmere, 2004, p152.

Wordsworth, Dorothy. *Recollections of a tour made in Scotland, AD 1803.* Edinburgh, David Douglas, 1894.

Wordsworth, Jonathan. *The music of humanity: a critical study of Wordsworth's "Ruined Cottage"; incorporating texts from a manuscript of 1799-1800.* London, Nelson, 1969.

Wordsworth, William. *The Fenwick notes of William Wordsworth.* Ed Jared Curtis, London, Bristol Classical Press, 1993.

Wordsworth, William. *The early letters of William and Dorothy Wordsworth, 1787-1805.* Ed DeSelincourt, Oxford, Clarendon, 1935.

Wordsworth, William. *Poems 1815.* (facsimile) Oxford, Woodstock, 1989.

Wordsworth, William. *The letters of William and Dorothy Wordsworth: the middle years.* Ed. DeSelincourt, Oxford, Clarendon, 1937.

Wordsworth, William. *Lyrical ballads, 1798.* Oxford, Woodstock, 1990.

Wordsworth, William. *The poetical works of William Wordsworth.* London, Longman, Rees, Orme, Brown, Green & Longman, 1832.

Wordsworth, William. *The Letters of William and Dorothy Wordsworth VIII A supplement of new letters.* Ed Alan G Hill, Oxford, Clarendon Press 1993.

Wordsworth, William. *A guide through the District of the Lakes in the north of England.* Kendal, Hudson & Nicholson, 5th Ed 1835.